# Devotion to the Miraculous Infant Jesus of Prague

Containing a History of its Origin and
Propagation with a Novena, a Litany
and Other Prayers

From approved sources

A Reprint of the Original 1898 Publication

Edited by J. M. Roberts, M. A. Lit.

Copyright © 2021 J. M. Roberts, M. A. Lit.

Civitas Dei Publications

All rights reserved.

ISBN: **9798720660062**

**Nihil Obstat.**

        Thomas L. Kinkead,

        *Censor Librorum*

**Imprimatur.**

        Michael Augustine,

        *Archbishop of New York*

New York, November 30, 1898.

## Contents

Original 1898 Preface .......................................................................... vii

POWERFUL NOVENA OF CHILDLIKE CONFIDENCE ........................... viii

1 The Church of Saint Mary of Victory at Prague ............................... 1

2 Origin of the Devotion ..................................................................... 3

3 Forgotten for Seven Years ............................................................... 5

4 The Infant Jesus of Prague and Father Cyrillus ............................... 8

5 The Infant Jesus of Prague and the Sick ........................................ 12

6 The Infant Jesus of Prague and Children ....................................... 19

7 The Infant Jesus of Prague and Sinners ......................................... 26

8 The Infant Jesus of Prague and Workers ....................................... 30

9 The Infant Jesus of Prague in Africa ............................................... 33

10 Other Favors Granted by the Infant Jesus of Prague .................. 35

11 The Infant Jesus of Prague Encircles the Globe. .......................... 38

12 Favors Granted by the Infant Jesus of Prague in the United States ................................................................................................... 43

13    Conclusion .................................................................................. 51

Prayers. ............................................................................................. 53

Litany of the Miraculous Infant of Prague ........................................ 56

PRAYERS TO BE RECITED BY A SICK PERSON ................................... 61

PRAYER FOR A HAPPY DEATH ........................................................... 62

Appendix ........................................................................................... 65

PRAYER OF THE REV. P. CYRILLUS A MATRE DEI, ............................. 67

# Original 1898 Preface

A few years ago, the devotion to the Infant Jesus of Prague was scarcely known in this country, though it had been practiced for over two centuries in Europe. In 1894 the first English account of the devotion appeared in a little book entitled "The Infant Jesus of Prague and Its Veneration," which set forth its history and cited some of the miracles that had taken place in connection with it. The book had a large sale and was the means of spreading the devotion throughout the land. Today, there is not a place where the Infant Jesus of Prague is not known and venerated, and his statues and pictures are found in many churches and convents, while medals and rosaries innumerable have been distributed among the faithful. The miracles performed and the favors granted by the Divine Infant to His clients in other lands have been repeated in this country, and a number of them will be found mentioned in these pages. May this book still further increase the devotion to the Miraculous Infant Jesus of Prague, and encourage the faithful to implore his aid with confidence in all their trials and difficulties.

# POWERFUL NOVENA OF CHILDLIKE CONFIDENCE

(This novena is to be said at the same time for nine consecutive hours.—Just one day.)

O Jesus, who hast said, "Ask and you shall receive, seek and you shall find, knock and it shall be opened to you, through the intercession of Mary, Thy Most Holy Mother, I knock, I seek, I ask that my prayer may be granted.
*(Make your request)*
O Jesus, who hast said, "All that you ask the Father in My Name, He will grant you, through the intercession of Mary, Thy Most Holy Mother, I humbly and urgently ask Thy Father in Thy Name that my prayer be granted.
*(Make your request)*
O Jesus, who hast said "Heaven and earth shall pass away but My Word shall not pass," through the intercession of Mary, Thy Most Holy Mother, I feel confident that my prayer will be granted.
*(Make your request)*

# 1 The Church of Saint Mary of Victory at Prague

On the 8th of November, 1620, the Austrian Emperor, Ferdinand II, gained a signal victory over the united Protestant armies at the battle of the White Mountain near Prague. This victory was of great importance to the Emperor and the royal house of Hapsburg, as well as to the Catholic cause in Bohemia. Father Dominic of Jesu-Maria, the superior of the discalced (bare-footed) Carmelites,--a monk famed no less for his remarkable intellectual gifts than for his rare piety—was in a particular manner connected with the favorable result of the battle. During the war this venerable priest carried on his person a picture of the birth of Christ, which he had found in the castle of Strakowitz. In this picture the Virgin Mother is represented as kneeling behind the Divine Child, while St. Joseph, holding a lantern in his left hand, stands back of his holy spouse; two shepherds are seen in the background. Heretics had pierced the eyes of all the figures. Before the battle began, Dominic holding his holy picture aloft, had urged the hesitating generals on to the conflict; chanting the *Salve Regina*, the imperial troops had marched to the combat, and when the battle was hottest, the enthusiastic religious spurred on the soldiers. "Mary! Mary!" became the battle cry, and after the rout of the enemy, arose the joyful shout "Victory! Victory!" Thankful to Heaven for his great success, and in recognition of the valuable services rendered by Father Dominic, Ferdinand founded several Carmelite monasteries: one at Vienna in 1622; one at Prague, 1624; and later one at Gratz. In Prague a Protestant prayer house was donated to the community, besides a chapel and a house. The church was solemnly blessed on the 4th of September in honor of "Saint Mary of Victory" (Maria de Victoria).

  This old Carmelite church is at the present day the parish church of Prague. One of the side altars is resplendent with burning candles, and on it is enthroned a beautiful little statue, the cynosure of all eyes. This statue, made of wax is 48 centimeters (about 19 inches) high and represents the Divine Infant Jesus. It is clothed in a costly royal mantle, and a beautiful crown, set with precious stones, rests on its head. Its right hand is raised in blessing, while its left hand holds the globe of sovereignty. This image with its benignant countenance, full of grace and majesty is known as *"The Infant Jesus of Prague."* Among the votive offerings which have been presented to it are twenty little dresses with mantles, all richly decorated, and some of them set with diamonds. Within the past fifteen years the devotion to this miraculous image has grown in a wonderful manner, and today the statue of the Infant Jesus of Prague may be seen in churches and chapels, in cloisters and schools, the world over. The Little King has taken up his abode among rich and poor, great and small. From Prague the devotion spread over Germany, Belgium, France, Holland, Luxemburg, Ireland and England, and thence made its way to America, Africa, India, and China. As a mighty tree springs up from the tiny mustard seed, so this pious devotion has grown from a small beginning to the greatest dimensions; it is no longer local or national, but as universal as the Church itself. Oh, that this Divine Infant might win to itself the hearts of all men!

# 2 Origin of the Devotion

The statue of the Infant Jesus of Prague originally came from Spain, the native country of that great reformer of the Carmelites, St. Teresa of Jesus. It was brought to Bohemia by Maria Mauriquez de Lara, a Spanish princess, in whose family the statue had been treasured highly as a miraculous heirloom. This noble lady presented the cherished image of the Divine Infant to her daughter, Princess Polizena, upon her marriage to Adelbert von Lobkowitz. After the death of the latter in 1623, his devout wife resolved to spend the remainder of her days in works of piety and charity. She was particularly generous to the Carmelites of Prague, who, after Emperor Ferdinand II, their founder, had changed his residence to Vienna, fell into such utter destitution, that at times they had scarcely bread enough to appease their hunger. The Princess resolved to put an end to their sad condition by giving them a treasure of permanent value. Accordingly, she brought to the monastery her beloved statue, and presented it to the monks with these prophetic words: "I hereby give you what I prize most highly in this world. As long as you venerate this image you shall not know want."

These words were literally fulfilled. The blessing of God entered the monastery, and the community prospered spiritually and temporally. But when the devotion to the Infant Jesus was relaxed God's blessing departed from the house.

The statue was set up in the oratory of the monastery, and twice a day the prescribed devotions were performed before it. The shrine soon became refuge for the monks when beset by difficulties of soul or body. The novices were particularly devout to the Holy Infant, and none of them more so than Cyrillus a Matre Dei. This young novice, who for years had suffered from aridity and dryness of spirit, found sudden relief from this torture by his devotion to the Infant Jesus.

# 3 Forgotten for Seven Years

The devotion to the Divine Infant was short-lived. In 1630 the novitiate of the Carmelites was removed to Munich, on account of the disturbances of the Thirty Years' War. When Brother Cyrillus and his associates had knelt for the last time before the venerable image, the Infant Jesus of Prague lost its most devout worshippers. The special devotions held before the image were gradually more and more neglected, and in the same measure the prosperity of the community declined and soon want and distress came again over the monastery.

King Gustavus Adolphus of Sweden, the inveterate foe of the Catholic religion, was devastating Germany, and the terror his name inspired spread to Prague. Nobles and citizens took to flight, and with them all the Carmelites but two left the city. On the 15th of November, 1631, the gates of Prague were thrown open, and over eighty Protestant preachers took possession of the churches in the city. The Carmelite monastery was plundered, and the two monks who had remained were made prisoners. Amid the confusion of their hasty flight, the religious had forgotten the sacred image, and the Protestant plunderers disdainfully threw the "Popish superstition," as they called it, into a heap of rubbish behind the high altar. Both hands of the Infant were broken off by the fall, but though made of wax it was not otherwise injured.

Here the miraculous Infant lay for seven years, forgotten by all, maimed, and deprived of all honor. When the Carmelites returned to Prague, in the continual struggle for the means of subsistence the miraculous image was entirely forgotten. As long as this neglect lasted the community suffered want and misfortune.

Ferdinand III discontinued the support granted by his father, and finally the religious became so poor that they could not even pay the rent for their fields and vineyards, and their lease was declared forfeited. They were now in the most deplorable condition. But still sadder days were in store for them. On account of the disorders caused by the war, the novices were sent to Munich a second time. Peace was made at Prague on the 13th of June, 1635, and thus the exhausted country had a chance to recover. But there was no peace and no recovery for the unfortunate religious; their miraculous Infant still lay disfigured and forgotten in the dust and rubbish. A novice happened to find the image one day, but without the least consideration, disdainfully cast it aside. Strange to say, a remarkable change came over this novice. Though he had been considered most promising in every respect, he now showed such evident signs of a want of vocation that his dismissal became necessary.

As long as the miraculous statue remained neglected a peculiar misfortune rested on the monastery. No prior or master of novices was able to hold out for the three years of the office; unbearable burdens and annoyances invariably caused them to resign their position. Even the other religious felt so uneasy in this convent that they asked to be transferred. The Provincial of the Order could not understand why God's blessing had fled from the monastery at Prague, nor why such severe afflictions were sent down upon it. This state continued seven years.

# 4 The Infant Jesus of Prague and Father Cyrillus

On the feast of Pentecost, 1637, Father Cyrillus a Matre Dei was sent by his superior from Munich to the convent of Prague. He was the very novice who, through his fervent devotion to the Holy Infant, had been delivered from a most annoying dryness of soul. Prague was again in danger of being overrun by the Protestant armies, and the religious sent most ardent supplications to Heaven that this new calamity might be averted. In this extremity Father Cyrillus remembered his former benefactor, and with the prior's consent he searched every nook and corner of the monastery, until he found the long-lost treasure, almost buried in dust. Full of joy and gratitude, he covered the statue with tears and kisses, and then placed it on an altar in the oratory. The long-forgotten devotions were now revived with renewed vigor. The religious laid bare their needs and their troubles before the Divine Infant, and many a one found there strength and consolation. Shortly after this the enemy withdrew from the city, and the monastery, which was in sore need, was in a most unexpected manner abundantly supplied with provisions. As in former years, Father Cyrillus was the most zealous disciple of the Holy Infant, and long after the other monks had left the monastery, he would remain kneeling before the lovely statue. On one occasion he distinctly heard the following words:

"Have pity on Me, and I will have pity on you. Give Me My hands, and I will give you peace. The more you honor Me, the more will I bless you."

The religious was awestruck at these words. He carefully examined the statue, for he had not before noticed that the hands of the Divine Infant were missing, owing to the mantle in which the figure was clad. Hastening to the prior, he besought him to have the image repaired. His pleadings were in vain; for the prior considered the community too poor for incurring such superfluous expenses. Cyrillus, however, did not waver, but implored God on his knees to send sufficient alms for the purpose of restoring the arms of the mutilated Infant.

His confidence was rewarded. Three days later he was summoned to the sick-bed of a wealthy man, who, having heard the history of the remarkable statue, at once gave 100 florins to Father Cyrillus for the purpose of repairing it. The prior, however, decided that it would be better to use the money in buying an entirely new statue, instead of having the old one repaired. This new statue had scarcely been put in place when it was broken to pieces by a falling candlestick. The old and mutilated image was evidently destined to continue an object of veneration in the monastery. The prior who had ordered its removal grew restless and melancholy, and resigned before the expiration of his term; this was generally considered a punishment inflicted by the Divine Infant.

His successor, Father Dominic of St. Nicholas, a virtuous man and later a most active missionary, found it impossible to fulfil Father Cyrillus's wish, owing to lack of funds. Cyrillus, full of perseverance, continued to ask God for help. One day a strange lady had him called to the church, and gave him a large sum of money. When he wished to thank her, she had disappeared; no one had seen her come or go. The happy religious then knelt down at the altar of Our Lady of the Scapular and offered his gratitude to Heaven. The prior, however, in view of the many needs of the monastery, allowed him to spend only a very small part of the sum for the repairing of the statue. This sum not proving sufficient, Father Cyrillus found himself as far as ever from attaining his object. Meanwhile, new afflictions visited the community; a pestilence broke out in the city, and several of the religious fell victims to it; the prior himself was attacked, and regained his health only after vowing to make every effort to propagate the devotion to the Holy Infant. The statue, however, remained in its mutilated condition, and Father Cyrillus shed many a tear of sorrow before his beloved Infant.

On one of these occasions he heard these words: "Place Me near the entrance of the sacristy and you will receive aid." He did so, and returned to his cell with new hopes springing up within him. Soon a stranger came to the sacristy, who offered to have the little image repaired at his expense. The prior gladly accepted his offer, and in a few days the repaired statue was exposed for veneration in the church. The Infant Jesus richly repaid the stranger for this good deed.

Thenceforth the statue of the Holy Infant became an object of special veneration throughout Prague. It is impossible to relate all the honor bestowed on the Infant Jesus of Prague during the past three centuries, not only in the capital of Bohemia, but also in many other cities; still more impossible would it be to recount the numerous miracles wrought by the Divine Infant among its faithful worshippers in all parts of the world. We shall recount but a few of them here.

# 5 The Infant Jesus of Prague and the Sick

The piety of the faithful has with good reason bestowed on the Divine Infant the title of the "Heavenly Physician." In the month of July, 1639, the Countess Elizabeth Kolowrat, ne Baroness von Lebkowitz, fell dangerously ill at Prague. Her sufferings became daily more intense, and finally she entirely lost her hearing and speech. Her physicians declared her case hopeless, and her end seemed at hand; but her husband, a devout worshipper of the Divine Infant, begged Father Cyrillus to bring the blessed statue to the bedside of his dying spouse. The priest held the statue before the agonized woman, who, unable to utter a word, covered it with kisses and promised to show her gratitude publicly if she should obtain relief in her sufferings. After blessing the sick woman, Father Cyrillus returned to the monastery, leaving the statue, however, at her bedside. A few moments after his departure, the Countess suddenly revived, she was able to speak and to hear, and she gained strength so rapidly that in a few days she could accompany her husband to his country seat. The happy and grateful lady was not unmindful of her promise made to the Divine Infant; she presented a golden crown, which at the present day still adorns the statue. Her husband, on his part, became a generous benefactor of the Carmelites throughout his life, and after his death, he left to the merciful Deliverer a silver lamp and a valuable shrine.

In the year 1733, a maiden of twenty-two years was lying at the point of death at Gratz, in Styria. A violent fever had seized her, and several physicians had in vain tried to check its ravages. Fortified with the last sacraments, the suffering girl was calmly awaiting her last moments. The members of a religious community sent her an exact copy of the miraculous statue. Casting her eyes upon the image, the girl confidently implored the help of the Divine Infant. She immediately fell into a deep slumber. On awaking, she exclaimed joyously: "I am cured; the Infant Jesus has restored my health; I wish to rise." The attendants, thinking that she was delirious, forced her to lie down until the physician came, who, to his great amazement, found her completely cured.

Five years later the physician of this same community was suffering from an incurable malady. He knew that there was no cure possible by earthly means, and he therefore asked the nuns to pray for him. One of them there upon sent him a picture of the Infant Jesus of Prague. The physician, with great confidence, implored the help of the Little King, and had a Mass said in His honor. Immediately his condition began to improve, and in a few days he was able to perform the duties of his profession.

All these facts, however, are far removed from us; we shall therefore relate some cures of our own time.

In the early part of November, 1892, a woman in Vienna was suffering from a severe attack of inflammation of the bowels. Being naturally delicate, she sank so fast that two physicians gave up all hope of saving her life. In this extremity, her relatives took refuge to the Infant Jesus of Prague by making a novena in His honor. A third physician, who had been summoned, declared the case not absolutely hopeless, but stated that a cure, if at all possible, would require three or four months. Despite his declaration, the woman was well in three or four days, and had regained sufficient strength to go about her household duties. She has not experienced the least symptoms of a relapse, and frequently sends up her thanks to the Heavenly Physician.

In 1891, M. de Laurens, a French nobleman living in Gourmes, went to Montpellier to have an abscess removed from his liver. When one of the physicians who was to treat him removed the bandages, he found no trace of the complaint. Astonished at this discovery, he exclaimed, "How could the abscess be removed without leaving a scar? I see none and still the evil has disappeared. Has Our Lady of Lourdes effected this cure?" The wife of M. de Laurens replied: "I can but attribute the cure to a novena made to the Infant Jesus of Prague in my husband's behalf in a Belgian convent." The physician, on hearing this explanation, declared that he regarded the cure a most wonderful one.

In January, 1891, a nun fell from the second story of the Benedictine convent of Estaires. The bones in one of her knees were so completely shattered that the physician declared the amputation of the entire leg absolutely necessary. This was, however, delayed until the unfortunate nun should regain sufficient strength. Meanwhile the abbess, having heard of the devotion to the Infant Jesus of Prague, instituted a novena and procured rosaries, pictures and medals of the Divine Infant. The wounded sister at once showed signs of improvement, and soon healthy flesh had overgrown the open knee, so that on the ninth day of the novena the nun was able to occupy her usual place at the chapel organ.

In August 1892, a French lady was at the point of death from an acute attack of peritonitis. The Carmelite nuns at Constance were asked to pray for her to the Infant Jesus of Prague. The nuns hastened to comply with this request, and also sent the suffering lady a little oil from the lamp which is kept burning continually before their statue of the Divine Infant. A marked improvement became noticeable at once, and in a short while, the lady had recovered completely.

In the same community a few years ago, eleven nuns were attacked by the influenza. The prioress, who was among the number, fell very sick, and a severe inflammation of the chest soon made her condition hopeless.

A novena to the Divine Infant was begun, but the sick nun grew worse, so that the Last Sacraments had to be administered to her. For seven days she hovered over the grave, and on the last day of the novena all of the nuns assembled in her room, momentarily expecting the fatal termination to her sufferings. One of the nuns felt inspired to bring the statue of the Infant Jesus to the bed side; immediately an improvement was noticed, and in a little time, the prioress was again in perfect health.

A man forty years old, who had a sister in the Carmelite convent at Meaux, was during an attack of typhoid fever, subject to fits of the greatest violence, so that at times he spat upon his attendants and even struck or bit them. This continued until he was shown a medal of the Divine Infant which was fastened to the curtains of his bed; he at once became meek as a lamb, and soon recovered completely.

About four years ago a most remarkable cure was effected in Belgium. An aged lady of sixty-seven years was suffering from anthrax, a disease which at first produces intense pain in the finger-tips and later destroys the finger-joints. The most famous physicians could not stop the ravages of the disease, and accordingly her only daughter, disconsolate on account of the severe sufferings of her dear mother, sent up most ardent prayers to God that He might grant her some relief. But God seemed not to hear her supplications, and one day she spoke to a relative of her fruitless prayers. The latter advised her to make a novena to the Infant Jesus of Prague. A novena of Masses was at once begun, while a picture of the Divine Infant was given to the sick woman, who received it with the most profound devotion. Her sufferings grew less from that moment, and the day after, her physician, to his amazement, noticed a great improvement. The charred finger-tips dropped off, and then the greatest miracle occurred: the fingers regained their shape and the nails grew on them as before. One of the joints which had dropped off, was sent to a university professor, who had been consulted in the case some time before, and he declared the cure inexplicable, viewed from a natural standpoint.

The devotion of the rosary of the Infant Jesus has been practiced for the last 200 years, frequently with most remarkable results. The prioress at the Carmelite convent at Prague, Sister Mary of All Saints, was for a number of years troubled with a great difficulty in breathing, so that rapid walking always brought on complete exhaustion. This evil was early in 1739 complicated by the appearance of catarrh, and during Holy Week, the prioress felt that her end was drawing near. Two days after Easter she felt especially weak. Despairing of human aid, she placed a picture of the gracious Infant upon her breast, and promised to recite the rosary in His honor for nine days. When she awoke the next morning after a quiet night, all pain had entirely disappeared, and she felt as though entering upon a new existence[1]

---

[1] This rosary is recited as follows: Our Father, etc. is recited 3

At a convent school near Mons, the solemn dedication of the statue of the Divine Infant of Prague was to take place in the chapel on the 27th of April, 1890. All preparations for the feast had been made by the Reverend Dean himself. 12 girls, dressed in white, were to represent the 12 years of Christ's infancy. The nuns, the parents and the children were all looking forward with joy to this great feast. In the midst of the preparations, one of the teachers was seized with a painful and dangerous disease, which rendered an immediate operation imperative. It seemed as if the festival day was to be turned into one of mourning. Nuns and pupils prayed by turns the rosary of the Infant Jesus for 12 consecutive hours; to the joy of all, the operation was performed successfully, the sick nun experienced neither pain nor fever, and in a short time she recovered completely.

Praise and honor to the dear Infant Jesus of Prague! Take courage, ye who are afflicted! When earthly physicians despair of curing or even relieving you, you still have the "Heavenly Physician" to rely upon, for He is the

---

times, in honor of the Holy Family; Hail Mary 12 times, in honor of the 12 years of our Divine Savior's infancy. Each Our Father is preceded by the words: "And the Word was made flesh," and before the first Hail Mary the words "And the word was made flesh and dwelt among us," are to be recited (300 days' indulgence. Pius IX., Aug. 9, 1855)

The Holy Infant revealed to a Carmelite nun, who died in the odor of sanctity, how agreeable this holy devotion is to Him. He promises special graces, particularly purity of heart and innocence, to all who carry this rosary on their person and recite it in honor of His holy infancy. This saintly nun saw the rosary of the Divine Infant encircled by the light of Heavenly glory as a sign of Our Lord's approval of the devotion.

"Resurrection and the Life." Address yourself with implicit confidence to the Divine Infant, and you will be sure to obtain your request, if it be to God's greater glory and your own salvation.

# 6 The Infant Jesus of Prague and Children

The propitious Infant has graces and blessing for all, but He seems to be particularly liberal of His favors to those children who have been recommended or dedicated to Him by Christian mothers.

At Prague, John Weidener, a boy of two years, became blind after an attack of smallpox. His mother for months had used remedy upon remedy without avail, and as a last resort she decided to ask the help of the Divine Infant. One day she left her poor little son, who was lying in his cradle eating a bunch of grapes, to attend the Holy Sacrifice of the Mass which was to be offered up for her intention on the altar of the Little King in the Carmelite church. During her absence, her little daughter had to take care of the blind boy. While thus engaged, the girl noticed that her brother opened his eyes toward the light, and when she saw him throw all the seeds of the grapes on the same spot, she felt certain that he had regained his sight. "Mother, Mother! John is no longer blind; he is cured!" she cried to her mother, who had just entered. The pious woman, having convinced herself that this was really the case, at once returned to the church to pour forth her thanks at the shrine of the Divine Infant.

At Prague, in the year 1752, John Nepomucene, the little son of the royal court physician, Joseph de Vignet, had the smallpox, which left him with an affliction of the eyes, and finally he became totally blind, despite the best of medical attendance. This was a hard blow for his good parents, who loved him dearly, but they did not despair. "Finding human help of no avail" thus the father relates, "We took or refuge to the merciful Infant Jesus, and brought our son to His shrine. The little boy had before been unable to endure the light, but in the church, it did not trouble him in the least, and during Mass he exclaimed, "Mamma, I can see! I see the Infant Jesus!" From that moment his eyes improved and all traces of the smallpox disappeared; his sight became clear, and he never afterwards experienced any trouble with his eyes."

At Eisendorf, in Silesia, a little boy had his left leg paralyzed, and became too weak to undergo medical treatment. His parents made a vow to attend the Holy Sacrifice of the Mass which was to be offered up for their intention by the Franciscan Fathers at Glatz, before the statue of the Infant Jesus, a copy of the one at Prague. When about to depart, the lame boy's grandmother said to him: "Well Felix, are you coming along? We are going to the Divine Infant." The boy, who for a long time had been unable to move, got up, and full of joy, began to run about the house. He was completely cured.

An infant but a few months old, while playing with a piece of money, swallowed it. The coin stuck in the windpipe and the child was almost choked. Its dismayed mother applied for help to the Holy Infant of Prague and promised to perform an act of charity in His honor if her child would be saved from death. Her prayer was heard, for the coin suddenly was thrown from the windpipe into the mouth, and the infant spat it out without difficulty.

At Mont-sur-Marchienne, a child of five years was brought to the brink of the grave by violent brain-fever. Death was already standing at the bed side of the little sufferer, his hands and feet were becoming cold and stiff, when his parents began a novena to the Infant Jesus of Prague. From the first, a remarkable change for the better was apparent in the condition of the sick child, and after several days it was brought to the chapel of the Carmelite nuns to thank the Heavenly Physician for his its recovery.

In June, 1890, a little girl became deaf, dumb, blind, and lame through meningitis. The most assiduous nursing and the best of medical care were of no avail; death seemed to be the sole relief for the suffering child. One of the girl's teachers went with several pious persons to the Carmelite church at Namur, to pray at the shrine of the Infant Jesus of Prague; she also began a novena with this intention. The poor girl showed signs of improvement on the fifth day, but her tongue remained paralyzed. The prayers were continued with greater fervor, and on the ninth day the child was quite well and could hear and speak.

In numerous instances sick children, whose recovery seemed impossible, have been restored to health by having the medal or the picture of the Infant Jesus of Prague placed on the diseased parts of their bodies. The medal bears a representation of the Divine Infant. It is generally joined to a small rosary, but it can also be obtained separately. All who wear it with confidence will find it of great efficacy. It is, however, particularly intended for children, that they may obtain the powerful blessings of their Divine Model, especially at the present time, when so many dangers threaten their innocence. For this reason there are engraved on it these words: "Holy Infant Jesus, Bless Us!"

We shall now relate a few cases where wonderful cures were obtained by the devout application of the medal or picture of the Holy Infant.

In an orphanage a girl of eight years had a very sore thumb. Some mortification set in, and it was thought necessary to have the thumb amputated. This was a hard trial for the little girl and a cause of great sorrow for the Superior, who had become the poor orphan's second mother. The other children were also inconsolable, for the suffering of their playmate seemed to be their own. The little girl edified all by her patience and resignation. "I suffer very much," she used to say, "But it is for the dear Infant Jesus." Everyone in the orphanage was directed to pray for her relief to the Infant Jesus of Prague; a burning candle was placed before His picture and a novena begun, while a medal of the Divine Infant was fastened to the sore thumb of the little girl. The mortification ceased on the first day, and in a short time the thumb had healed. The recovery of the girl produced the greatest rejoicing in the institution. All the children were enrolled in the Sodality of the Infant Jesus, and vied with one another in honoring the little King.

At Ghent, a boy of nine years, who was a general favorite, had through carelessness run a steel pen into the thumb of his right hand. The injury remained unnoticed at first, but soon a large ulcer formed on the thumb, and the swelling extended so that it seemed that the whole hand would be lost. Pious friends recommended the devotion to the Infant Jesus of Prague. Prayers were at once offered up with the greatest fervor and confidence, and a medal of the Divine Child was fastened to the wound. The prayers were heard, for in a few days the swelling disappeared and the boy was out of all danger.

## Devotion to the Miraculous Infant Jesus of Prague

A little girl, in El..., who was the joy and happiness of her parents, was taken sick with croup, that treacherous disease which so often cuts short the lives of tender children. Heavy breathing and repeated gasping showed her condition to be most precarious. The anxious parents placed their sole reliance on the merciful Infant Jesus, having often heard of wonderful cures through His aid. A medal of the Little King was laid upon their child's breast, while they began a novena before His picture. As in hundreds of other cases, the sick child at once showed signs of improvement, and before the close of the devotion, every trace of the illness had disappeared.

In 1891, at Aries (France), little Stephen Gay, while playing with his comrades, fell and injured his knee. Fearing to alarm his parents, he made no mention of his injury; but after a few hours he was compelled to do so on account of the excessive pain. A physician upon examining the knee found it to be out of joint; he gave the boy's leg several severe pulls in order to re-adjust the knee, and then ordered cloths dipped in lead water to be placed on it every ten minutes, remarking that the cure would be long and tedious. On account of this, a novena to the Infant Jesus of Prague was begun by the uneasy parents; the boy's grandmother in her simple, childlike faith, took care, whenever the poultices were changed, to touch the inflamed knee with a picture of the Divine Infant. In a few days all pain had disappeared. The physician, expecting an accumulation of water in the knee, decided to remove it by means of a plaster; but when he called again on the last day of the novena, he found the knee in a perfectly healthy condition.

The wife of a poor coachman had an incurable sore on one of her legs, so that she was unable to walk. Her eldest son, a child of ten years, one day received a penny for a present; he decided to spend it in a way which would benefit his invalid mother. "Perhaps the Infant Jesus will cure her," he said to himself. And accordingly, he went to purchase a picture of the Infant Jesus of Prague. Running home full of joy, he exclaimed to his mother, "Mamma, place this picture upon your sore; the Infant Jesus will certainly cure you." "Do not speak thus, my child," replied the poor woman. "It would be disrespectful to put the holy picture to such use." "Mamma, I beg you, do not refuse: the Divine Infant will not take offence, but He will cure you, as He has cured so many others by this means." Finally the mother consented, and instantly her pains, heretofore intolerable, disappeared. Her restoration to health was so rapid and so complete that her physician could not but attribute it to a miracle.

In recalling to mind the touching incidents during Our Savior's life on earth, we cannot but notice His great love for children. "Suffer little children to come unto Me," He said. And at these tender and loving words, the crowds surrounding the Divine Redeemer parted, and allowed pious mothers to bring their offspring to Him, that He might bless them. And Jesus, raising His hands, implanted in those young hearts the fruitful seed of all virtues. What became later of those fortunate children, who had been blessed in such a particular manner? Tradition tells us that they ever afterwards showed great wisdom, became zealous apostles and lived most saintly lives. Such are the bountiful fruits of Jesus' blessing.

Dear children, you who read these lines, honor very devoutly the Infant Jesus of Prague, and dedicate yourselves to Him with all your heart. Lay before him your childish desires and your little troubles, and recommend to Him your dear parents, sisters and brothers. Christian parents, induce your children to wear with respect and devotion the medal of their Divine Model, who Himself became a child for the sake of us all. Let your children press to their lips the image of the Holy Infant, while they recite with fervor: "Holy Infant Jesus, bless us!" The good and kind Infant Jesus, who loves them so tenderly, will bless them, as He blessed the children during His life on earth; He will, in like manner, make them wise, pious, obedient and will overwhelm them with graces.

# 7 The Infant Jesus of Prague and Sinners

"I am not come to call the just, but sinners," said our Divine Savior. And the Infant Jesus of Prague has given repeated proofs of His infinite mercy to sinners. We shall cite but a few examples.

One day a man, who for years had been estranged from God, came into the confessional. "Father," he said to the priest, "I really do not know why I came here, because I do not repent of my sins and have not resolved to amend." The confessor tried to touch his heart, but his efforts were in vain. "At least," he said finally, "go to the shrine of the Infant Jesus and offer Him this simple prayer: "O Divine Infant, enlighten my mind and help me to have the proper dispositions for making a good confession." The man obeyed, and his heart heretofore so hard and obdurate, was at once softened. Touched by divine grace, he shed tears and made a most humble confession. After receiving absolution, he left the confessional blessing the divine mercy of the Infant Jesus.

Out of curiosity a woman once went to the shrine of the Infant Jesus of Prague. She inspected closely the silk mantle, the precious diadem and the golden globe in the Holy Infant's hand. But she could not see His countenance. Seized with fear, she began to tremble, her conscience made her most bitter reproaches, and she recognized that it was her sins which hid from her sight the divine countenance. Full of remorse, she hastened to make her confession, and then returned to the shrine. Now she saw distinctly the smiling features of the Divine Infant; but only for an instant, for a cloud suddenly concealed them again. The woman was seized with a new fear, and asked Our Lord why his countenance was again hidden from her. "Because you have omitted a sin in your confession," was the answer. She retraced her steps to the confessional, and after having completely cleansed her soul, she was able clearly to see the face of the miraculous image. The woman herself has under oath given this account of her conversion.

At Mons in Belgium the father of a family neglected his religious duties, and had not been to the sacraments for forty years. It was in vain that his wife and children put forth most strenuous and persistent efforts to bring him back to God. In 1889 he became seriously ill, but even then he would not think of religion. One, two, three novenas were made to the Infant Jesus of Prague; on the third day of the last one, the hardened sinner suddenly asked for a priest. He then made a sincere confession, received the last sacraments of the Church, and died peacefully.

In 1893 a young maiden of Bourges was lying at the point of death; she had always been indifferent in matters of religion, and even now manifested no desire for conversion. Her mother requested the Carmelite nuns of Bourges to pray for her before the Infant Jesus of Prague.

Feeling confident that these prayers would be successful, the mother admonished the daughter to prepare for a good death; she was met however, with an absolute refusal. A priest, who had been called to try to save this poor soul, came to the house a few minutes later. Contrary to his expectations, the dying girl received him willingly, and even promised to make her confession on the next day. But her last agony set in during the day, and she lost the power of speech. The nuns at the convent redoubled their prayers; the priest returned, but was told that he was too late. Nevertheless, he approached the bed side, and thanks to the merciful Infant Jesus, the maiden suddenly regained sufficient strength to make her confession. Soon after, the agony set in again, and the girl expired.

In the year 1894 a certain young man was leading a most sinful life, casting all admonitions of priests and friends to the winds. His sister spoke to a nun at Metz of her fruitless attempts to convert him. The nun advised her to make a novena to the Infant Jesus of Prague and also gave her a medal, which the loving sister sewed into her brother's clothing. A change came over the young man on the first day of the novena; that evening he came home at an early hour, and contrary to his practice greeted the members of the household in a most cordial manner. Before the close of the novena he had returned to an upright and virtuous life.

On the fourth of February, 1895, there occurred in the city of Luxembourg a remarkable conversion. A young man, having failed to obtain a much-coveted position, became addicted to drink, and for ten years neglected all his religious duties. He was seized by a severe illness, and his case soon became hopeless. At the least mention of religion, he flew into a violent passion, and soon he drove away the brother who was nursing him and was trying to bring him back to a sense of his duties. In the next room a Carmelite nun was attending his grandmother, who was 96 years old. The nun at times approached the bed side of the sick man, but he also refused to listen to her. "If no miracle takes place," the relatives were heard to say repeatedly, "he will die without a priest." The obstinate sinner was recommended to the prayers of the Carmelite nuns; the nuns sent a small gospel book and a medal of the Infant of Prague and also promised to publish it if their prayers should be heard. The book and the medal were placed under the sick man's pillow, and the Litany of the Holy Name of Jesus was recited for him. Three nights later the poor sinner suddenly cried out: "Drive away the black men in that corner, and also the gray ones on the other side!" "There is no one here," said the sister who had come from the next room. "Yes there is; chase them away—there, in the corner!" "I cannot, for I see no one." The sick man earnestly repeated his request. "O, a little child of three years is coming and driving the black men away, O, who is that child?" "It is the Infant Jesus," replied the good sister. The man continued to speak of the Holy Infant for the remainder of the night. The nurse took advantage of his changed disposition and had a priest summoned. The latter was received in a friendly manner, and with little difficulty succeeded in reconciling the erring soul with God. The repentant sinner experienced a heavenly joy, and expired peacefully on the 9th of February.

O Divine Infant Savior, who camest into the world to save poor sinners, have mercy on those who are dear to us, and do not permit them to depart this life without being reconciled to Thee!

# 8 The Infant Jesus of Prague and Workers

The only-begotten Son of God spent the years of His youth in labor and toil, and it is therefore not astonishing that He should show particular favor to the laboring classes. Times out of number have poor workmen, finding themselves and their families destitute and beset by difficulties, applied to the Divine Infant, and never have they failed to obtain the desired help.

A printer, Mathew Adam Hoeger by name, was by a series of misfortunes and his failure to obtain work brough to the verge of financial ruin. He prayed confidently to the Infant Jesus, received Holy Communion in His honor, and presented a missal, printed by himself, to the chapel of the miraculous image. The Little Savior in a short time helped the poor man out of his difficulties; for he was entrusted with the printing of a work which brought him in three thousand marks.

Edward Joseph Schmeidt, of Bodenstadt, became completely deaf in 1893. Being, moreover, subject to severe headaches, he could not perform any work, and soon found himself reduced to the direst want. In this extremity he set up in his house an image of the Infant Jesus of Prague and began to venerate it most fervently. God's bountiful blessings seemed to come into the man's house with the image, for he regained his hearing, and everything commenced to prosper; his business has revived and he enjoys perfect health. He has made known this occurrence, so that others in trouble or in poverty may follow his example and apply to the Divine Infant for assistance.

A sculptor in Prague had received an order to make a statue of the Holy Infant, which was in all respects, except the material, to be a fac-simile of the original in the Carmelite church. To get as good a likeness as possible, he frequently visited the church and the sweet expression of the Divine Infant touched him so greatly, that he begged the little King with great confidence always to supply him with sufficient employment for the support of his family. His request was granted; for he had not yet completed the statue when orders for copies came in from all sides, and he was kept busy supplying them.

A Laborer in Munster, Westphalia, who earned very low wages was unable to meet the demands of his creditors. Hearing of the wonders of the Infant Jesus of Prague, he said to himself: "I will apply to the Divine Infant, for just as it is easy to obtain anything from a child, so I think Our Lord will the sooner hear me if I venerate His holy infancy." He made a novena to the Holy Child, and on the last day received a gift of one hundred marks from a pious person. Encouraged by this success he began ta second novena; at its close the news reached him that he had one two hundred and twelve marks in a lottery. Another proof of the Divine Infant's power and mercy was given him some time later.

One of his creditors had a mortgage on his house, and declared that he would sell the building. A third novena to the powerful Infant of Prague was at once commenced by the pious man, and as a result the creditor remitted the whole amount of the debt. Furthermore the man received a present of forty marks on the same day.

Christian workmen into whose hands this little book may happen to fall, if you are out of work, or if you receive low wages, approach with simplicity and confidence the loving Heart of Him who out of love for you toiled as a laborer in the workshop of St. Joseph. Expose your cares and afflictions to the Little Friend of sufferers, and you will be certain to find help. Place no trust in the empty words and the vain promises of a false world. Jesus Christ alone can solve the social problem; go to Him and He will enlighten you.

# 9 The Infant Jesus of Prague in Africa

Most touching reports have been received of the sincere devotion with which the native children in Africa regard the Infant Jesus of Prague and lay before Him their wants. In the interior of Western Africa, amidst fierce tribal hostilities, the Little King has established His rule amongst the newly converted people of the Congo. His palace is nothing but a rude hut with a straw roof, but He has many devout worshippers, and the Fathers of the Holy Ghost relate many cases where prayers were immediately heard.

Father Schmit writes: "In September, 1894, the Bambembes, our neighbors, according to custom set the long dry grass of the plains on fire. Our large Loango hut was in imminent danger of destruction by the flames; the frightened neighbors had taken to flight and the efforts of a lay-brother and myself were as nothing against the approaching conflagration. We saw that human help was impossible, and we therefore had recourse to the Infant Jesus of Prague. At once the wind changed and drove the flames in the opposite direction, so that our humble but indispensable abode was saved.

"A few weeks later the Holy Infant averted from us a still greater calamity. Ngoma, a neighboring chief, made an attempt on the life of one of our missionaries. Like a wild beast he pursued the poor Father, who fortunately reached a place of safety just in time. I applied for help to the military station at Londima, which was four days' journey distant from us. But the chief might destroy the entire mission, and kill all the missionaries, before help could reach us from Londima. We therefore besought the Infant Jesus of Prague to protect us. We had scarcely begun a novena in His honor when Ngoma repented, and of his own accord came to us to ask pardon and to make reparation. Thus the Almighty Infant had suddenly made a meek lamb out of a bloodthirsty tiger."

While Father Schmit was away on his first apostolic journey to the unknown inhabitants of the neighboring mountains, the baptized native children assembled every evening before the Holy Infant's shrine to pray for their absent Father. Their childish prayers bore good fruit: the missionary was welcomed everywhere, he succeeded in saving many souls, and he brough back with him to Buanza three children whom he had liberated from slavery. "In all our cares," thus Father Schmit closes his account, "we appeal to the Infant of Prague, and never in vain."

# 10 Other Favors Granted by the Infant Jesus of Prague

Joseph Hofer, a boy from Aschau, in Austria, one day ran away from school and home to escape punishment. His mother was beside herself with grief, for during three long years nothing was heard of him. About this time the unfortunate woman met a friend in the city of Linz and told her of the loss of her child. The friend at once advised her to have recourse to the miraculous Infant Jesus in the Carmelite church. The afflicted woman went to lay her sorrow before the Divine Child, and asked Him to restore her lost son. This was on the boy's names-day, Thursday, March 19, 1739. On the following day the woman renewed her petition during the holy sacrifice of the Mass. But what had become of the runaway boy? For three years he wandered from place to place, begging for his daily bread and often suffering the greatest want. Clad in rags and covered with vermin, he reached the Maria-Zell in Styria. At the very moment when his mother was offering her prayers to the Holy Infant at Linz, he had a dream, admonishing him to turn his steps homeward. He did so, and two weeks later, on a Friday, he reached his native place. While he was resting before the castle of Aschau, his mother happened to pass by; she instantly recognized her long-lost boy! "Come with me; I know who has brought you back!" Soon after she went with the boy to Linz to offer her heartfelt thanks before the shrine of the Holy Infant; she related there these facts and declared herself willing to testify to them under oath.

Up to the 15th of June, 1889, there had not been any convent of the Carmelites in Luxemburg, that land so truly religious and so devoted to the Mother of God. Providence had decreed that the Infant Jesus of Prague and its zealous adorer Father Cyrillus should be the cause of this foundation. It so happened that a daughter of the seraphic St. Theresa, who in 1874 had entered a Carmelite convent in the Rhenish provinces, but who during the Kulturkampf resided in Roermond with some other Sisters, read that Father Cyrillus was born in Luxemburg, on January 23, 159. For years it had been this nun's most ardent desire to see a convent of her community established in Luxemburg, her native city, and this discovery indicated to her how her wish might be realized. With the greatest devotion she prayed: "Father Cyrillus, if you will assist in the establishment of a Carmelite convent in your birthplace, we will do everything in our power to spread the devotion to the Infant Jesus of Prague." The present Carmelite convent at Luxemburg, dedicated to the Infant Jesus, is a visible proof that this prayer was heard. The foundation of a convent seemed impossible in human estimation, but prayer surmounts all obstacles. On the 15th of June, 1889, four nuns left Roermond to found the new convent. The first postulant who entered the new institution had formerly occupied herself with artistic embroidering. She now employs her talent in honor of the Divine Infant, by adorning His images with most beautiful dresses, which are being sent to all parts of the world. The new convent was completed the 25$^{th}$ of December, 1893, thanks to the Divine Infant, whose blessing on the work was continually apparent, and who frequently sent material assistance in a most unexpected manner. Above the entrance to the convent there stands a large statue of the Infant Jesus of Prague. The miraculous statue adorns also the chapel, the oratory, and the novitiate. In this institution the words of the Holy Infant have been verified: "The more you honor Me, the more will I bless you."

# 11 The Infant Jesus of Prague Encircles the Globe.

An old book, printed in 1761 at Kempt, contains these passages: "All who approach the miraculous statue and pray there with confidence, receive assistance in danger, consolation in sorrow, aid in poverty, comfort in anxieties, light in spiritual darkness, streams of grace in dryness of soul, health in sickness, and hope in despair. From its beautiful eyes dart sparks of heavenly love; its smiling lips offer us spiritual riches, and its beauty conquers all hearts.

"No colic is so painful, no fever so violent, no malady so dangerous, no peril so great, no tumor so malignant, no insanity so raving, no complaint so irritating, no assault of Satan so furious, no pestilence so infectious, no swelling so serious, as not to be dispelled or cured by this Blessed Child. The Holy Infant puts an end to enmities, frees prisoners, saves those who are condemned to death, brings obstinate sinners to repentance, and blesses childless parents with offspring. In short He is become all to all."

In thanksgiving for the numerous graces and cures received at the hands of the Divine Infant, the miraculous statue at Prague was solemnly crowned in the year 1655, on the Sunday after Easter. Even then the feast of the Holy Name of Jesus was the principal feast of the Divine Infant, and the Litany of the Holy Name the most favorite prayer of His worshippers.

But such an excellent devotion could not be confined to one place; it was destined to spread from city to city and from country to country. The first copy of the miraculous statue, made like the original of wax, and touched to it after completion, was place in the chapel of the Carmelite nuns of St. Joseph in Prague. These pious women celebrated the entry of their Little King on the 25th of November, 1737, and from that time they made every possible effort to spread the honor and glory of His Name. Their favorite occupation, outside of their church duties, consisted in coloring the images and dressing them in silk, and in this way they helped to spread the devotion to Him far and wide. Almost innumerable are the pictures which are ornamented and distributed yearly by the nuns of this convent and by those of Gratz, Gmunden, and other communities. The Holy Infant also received a hearty welcome in the other convents of Prague, and numerous copies of His miraculous statue were made of wood or of wax, and then touched to the original.

In 1750 the royal court of Lisbon, Portugal, sent to Prague for a number of statues of the Infant Jesus. The statues were forwarded at once and distributed among the members of the court. One of them, however, was given to the Carmelite Fathers, in order that they might place it in their church for public veneration. This was done in a most solemn manner on the 17th of June, 1750, in the presence of the queen, two princes, and the whole court. The devotion to the Infant Jesus of Prague was soon spread all over Portugal.

About the same time statues of the Divine Infant had made their way to Vienna, Gratz, Linz, and Rome. Soon after this the statues were also to be found in many localities of Germany, Hungary, Saxony, Poland, France, Italy, Sicily, Malta, and Spain. Even to India and China and the farthest corners of the earth zealous Carmelites carried with them these lovely images, and thus spread the devotion to the Holy Infant. Numerous oil paintings, engravings, woodcuts, and medals of the Divine Infant were also produced.

Father Ildephonsus, General of the Carmelites, was especially active in extending the devotion. He always carried a picture of the Infant Jesus on his person, and on one occasion was miraculously saved from shipwreck by imploring His assistance. It was ordained that in all convents of Our Lady of Mount Carmel, whether of men or women, a statue of the Holy Infant should be set up for veneration. St. Teresa of Jesus, the celebrated reformer of the Carmelite Order, was very fond of this devotion. The blessed Crescentia of Kaufbeuern also possessed a statue of the Infant Jesus of Prague, which she had adorned with a beautiful dress; this statue became a source of great blessing to the poor Franciscan nuns, and the devotion to the Divine Infant has been zealously fostered by them to this day. Blessed Clement Maria Hofbauer was another ardent worshipper of the Divine Infant, and always had a statue of the Little King in his room.

The devotion to the Infant Jesus of Prague had thus reached its zenith about the middle of the eighteenth century, but the disastrous Seven Years' War not only checked its progress, but came near crushing it. Under

Emperor Joseph II, seventy churches, chapels, and convents in Prague alone were confiscated and closed, among others the monastery of the Carmelites attached to the church of St. Mary of Victory. The church itself was made the parish church on the 25th of September, 1784. The veneration of the Infant Jesus, however, at no time ceased entirely, and when in 1879 the church and the shrine were renovated, the devotion to the Divine Infant was triumphantly restored. Twelve convents in Prague had the happiness of harboring the lovely statue for a longer or shorter period, and they all vied with one another in showing it all the honor possible.

From this triumphant revival of the devotion dates the immense progress it has made at the present day. Never before have statues, pictures, rosaries, and medals been sent to all parts of the world in such large numbers. The veneration of the miraculous image has attained the greatest development in France, Belgium, and the Netherlands. The statue has been solemnly installed in many churches and the Little King has everywhere been received with the greatest enthusiasm. Individual families even, rich and poor, strive to possess the blessed image. The Sisters of the Assumption have introduced the devotion into all their institutions in France, Spain, and England. The convents of the Visitation bear as great a love to the Divine Infant as do the one hundred and twenty French Carmelite convents and their thirty Belgian houses. In German Lorraine the Infant Jesus of Prague was heartily welcomed in 1894 in most of the convents and schools of the Sisters of St. Chretienne of Metz. The Dominican and Borromaean nuns at Treves, Boppart, Kreuznach, etc., as well as the Sisters of Christian Doctrine, likewise venerate the Little King.

The Friend of Children finds His most devoted worshippers in schools and orphanages. This is especially the case among the young students at Bordeaux, who have become completely enamored of the Holy Infant, the sweetest of children. Their love and devotion have been frequently repaid by special favors. A shrine has been set up by them near their country-house at Bordeaux where they spend their holidays, and thus the Infant Jesus of Prague has a chapel of His own for public worship. In 1892 the Franciscan nuns brought statues of the Divine Infant to Norway, and in 1893 some were sent to Boston and New Orleans, to Brazil, Chile, China, Japan, and to Gabon in Africa. Missionaries and nuns recite their devotions before the statue of the Holy Infant in distant Australia. In the French sections of the Dominion of Canada the miraculous statue may be found almost everywhere.

In the United States this charming devotion has grown most rapidly during the past two years, and statues, medals, and pictures of the Divine Infant are being sent to all sections of the country. In the city of New York the Little King has taken up His abode in several churches and convents; in the Church of the Most Holy Redeemer, in Third Street, the miraculous statue, clad in costly garments and encased in a beautiful shrine, is an object of special veneration, and on all days of the week devout suppliants may be seen kneeling before the Holy Infant and imploring His help.

Thus the Infant Jesus of Prague is known and worshipped in almost all countries on the globe. And everywhere the promise He made to His first disciple, Father Cyrillus, has been fulfilled: "The more you honor Me, the more will I bless you."

## 12 Favors Granted by the Infant Jesus of Prague in the United States

We subjoin a number of cases which have occurred in our own country, and in which the cure of soul or body and other favors were obtained through the invocation of the Infant Jesus of Prague. As in most of the occurrences already cited, all details which might lead to the identification of the persons concerned are omitted; they are, however, fully known to the publisher of this little book, and he is able to vouch for the truth of the facts related here.

*A Deathbed Conversion*

In April, 1891, a young Protestant in New York, who had for years been convinced of the truth of the Catholic religion, was with the help of the Holy Infant converted on his deathbed. The parents of this young man, who were members of a secret society, had not lived together for a great number of years. This latter circumstance proved a drawback in the young man's education. When he was sixteen years old, his mother obtained for him a situation as messenger for a man who was a stranger to them. While thus employed, the boy, though himself ignorant of the fact, was assisting a band of thieves in the systematic robbery of hotels. He was arrested with his employers and, despite the repeated avowal of his innocence, sentenced to seven years' imprisonment at Sing Sing. He accepted his doom meekly, and in prison soon became interested in Catholic worship. The close confinement in a short time undermined his health, and he gradually fell a victim to consumption, so that after six years his mother obtained his release. He had for several years desired to join the Catholic Church, and now on his deathbed he sent his mother to a certain hospital in the city, where in earlier days he had several times visited, to bring one of the nuns to his bed-side. The nun took with her a picture of the Infant Jesus of Prague, and on the way she repeatedly implored the Holy Infant to assist her. She saw that the young man was near his end, and therefor exhorted him to prepare for eternity, giving him the picture of the Holy Infant. He clasped it devoutly in his thin hands, his languid eyes shone with the fire of heavenly grace, and turning to his mother he said: "Now I shall save my soul." A priest was then brought by the nun; the dying young man listened devoutly to the instructions of the good Father, and after due preparation received holy Baptism, as well as the Last Sacraments of the Church. He died peacefully, pressing the picture of the Divine Infant to his breast. His mother, though a Protestant, had him buried with all the rites of the Catholic Church, and even made a donation to the hospital for the offering up of prayers and Masses for the repose of his soul, and for the support of sick persons. Unfortunately, she has not up to the present carried out her promise of becoming a Catholic, which she had given her dying son, owing to an oath binding her to the secret societies. The sisters, however, are confident of effecting her conversion by continued prayers to the Infant Jesus.

## *A Woman's Conversion*

In the year 1888 the solemn coronation of the statue of the Infant Jesus of Prague took place in the hospital above referred to. A Jesuit priest, who was at that time among the patients in the institution, delivered a touching sermon on the occasion. One of the inmates, a Protestant woman, was particularly affected by the priest's words, and as a result she fervently begged God for the grace of conversion. She sent her two children with offerings to the Little King: one of them, a girl of eight years, presented Him with a diamond ring, while the other, a boy of ten years, brought some point lace in an envelope bearing his signature. The devout woman prayed continually for light, and after some time she was received into the bosom of the true Church. She was confirmed by His Grace Archbishop Corrigan in the vestry of the hospital chapel.

## *Miraculous Cure of an Italian*

About the same time a poor Italian was lying in the same institution, suffering from a dangerous wound on one of his legs. The suppuration from the wound extended to the hip-joint, and the unfortunate man was looked upon as a certain victim of death. He had been strengthened for the journey into eternity by a worthy reception of the Last Sacraments, and on three evenings the sisters in attendance had prepared a shroud for him, thinking he would die during the night. While everyone was thus expecting his last moments, the Jesuit Father referred to above visited the sick man and spoke to him of the miraculous Infant and he placed a picture of the Little King in his hand. The devotion to Christ's holy infancy is widespread in Italy, and the sick man, though unable to read the prayers on the picture, at once grasped their meaning, and began to utter prayers to the Holy Infant in his native tongue. To the surprise of all, the wound on his leg began to heal, and after some time he left the hospital cured, blessing and thanking the Divine Infant for his wonderful recovery.

## *A Woman's Sudden Recovery*

In the year 1892 a woman in the same institution had to undergo a most difficult operation for the third time. She was at first considered out of danger, but stagnation of the blood set in unexpectedly in the right leg. The leg was encased and placed in a high position, and the suffering woman had to retain this uncomfortable posture for three weeks during the hottest days of summer. One day Sister N. visited her and found her complaining to God that the numerous masses and prayers offered by her had not relieved her suffering. Sister N. advised her to pray to the Infant Jesus of Prague, and told her to place implicit trust in His assistance. The sick woman, having obtained a picture of the Infant Jesus of Prague, at once began a novena in His honor. When ten days later, Sister N., who had herself been slightly indisposed in the meantime, again went to visit the woman, she found the bed vacant. The attending sister told her that the occupant had prayed almost incessantly to the Divine Infant, never for a moment suffering His picture to leave her hands. Her great fervor was wonderfully rewarded, for she was able to go home in a few days perfectly cured. Since her recovery she has written twice to the hospital, stating that she was in perfect health.

## *The Divine Infant Banishes Avarice*

In the city of New York, there lived a widowed lady, who although possessing a fortune of seventy-five thousand dollars, was a victim to the most niggardly greed.

She led a wretched life, and often deprived herself of necessities in order to save money. When the infirmity of old age overtook her, she refused to make any preparation for death, either by having a priest called, or by making a disposal of her wealth. Well-meaning friends frequently visited her, but could effect nothing, and often had to spend their own money for the support of this truly poor rich woman. One of the members of a religious community became interested in her and made several fruitless attempts to induce her to prepare for eternity. But exhortation and prayer seemed powerless against the demon of avarice. On Christmas, a rainy and chilly day, the sister felt herself urged to visit the old woman again; though suffering from a severe cold herself, she hesitated not a moment, but went at once, taking holy water as well as a medal and a picture of the Divine Infant along with her. Approaching the bed side, the sister hung the medal about the woman's neck, and placed the picture on her breast, sprinkled the room with holy water, and began to pray. Several persons who happened to be in the room joined the prayers; in a little while the woman was heard to utter a word now and then, and finally she prayed louder than the rest. She then asked for a Mass to be said for a happy death, and also requested that a priest be sent to hear her confession. On the next day she made her last will and disposed of her property. Having thus freed herself from all earthly concerns, she spent the three remaining weeks of her life in prayer and meditation, frequently in company with the good sister, who had, with the Holy Infant's help, succeeded in softening her heart. It may be mentioned that the woman's conversion was effected on the day of Christ's Nativity, and her burial took place on the feast of His most holy Name.

*The Holy Infant Grants Relief in Suffering*

In a Catholic hospital in the state of New Jersey, the Infant Jesu of Prague has in several instances granted unexpected help. One of the attending nuns was for a long time suffering from a tumor on her side, which by degrees assumed an alarming character, while its position made an operation well-nigh impossible. In the measure in which the chances of obtaining human aid grew less, the reliance of the suffering nun in the assistance of the Divine Infant increased. She began a novena in His honor, and at once her condition improved, so that the operation could be performed with ease, and her recovery followed in a very short time.

Mr. W., a convert, was a patient in the same hospital, suffering most intense pains from a chronic inflammation of the bladder. All medicines failed to lessen his terrible torments, and accordingly he applied to the Divine Infant for relief. His prayer was heard, for after making a novena, his sufferings became endurable, and he experienced great patience and resignation in God's Holy Will.

In the same ward with Mr. W., there lay a man who had been completely paralyzed by a spinal disease. He was unable even to eat alone, and several physicians declared his case incurable. Mr. W. exhorted this man to address himself to the Holy Infant. The two men began a novena together and also decorated a picture of the Little King with flowers. During the devotion the paralyzed man showed signs of improvement and after a short time was restored to health.

A gentleman in the same city was in danger of losing a most remunerative position, owing to a painful disease of his eyes. All medicines proved of no avail, and the man awaited with dread the moment when he would have to give up the means of earning his livelihood. At the hospital one day, he explained his sad position to a nun, who told him of the many favors bestowed by the Infant Jesus of Prague on His devout worshippers. Full of confidence, the man invoked the Holy Infant's help in a novena, and soon his eyes were strong and in a healthy condition.

## *Unexpected Recovery of a Jewish Woman*

A Jewish woman had to undergo a very dangerous operation in the same hospital just referred to. Two days after the operation, symptoms of blood poisoning appeared, and the patient's body swelled to such an extent that the bandages had to be cut. The house surgeon visited her at ten o'clock in the evening, and declared that the woman would not possibly live beyond midnight. Perceiving the utter impossibility of saving the patient's life, by the resources of human knowledge, the nuns with so much greater confidence asked the Infant Jesus of a proof of His almighty power. Candles were lit before the miraculous statue in the chapel, while a picture of the Divine Infant was placed under the woman's pillow. At midnight a sudden change took place in her condition: the swelling subsided, her strength returned, the improvement continued from hour to hour, and next morning several physicians declared her cured.

## *Sickness and Poverty Dispelled by the Holy Infant*

The following is taken from a letter written to a priest in 1895 by a devout Catholic in Michigan: "The Infant Jesus has become our all. Our devotion to Him began in the following manner: last fall we were in great want, as my sickness rendered me unable to work, while my wife lost her employment through calumny. In these reduced circumstances our youngest child fell seriously ill, so that a physician declared it would not live for a day. We could not possibly pay the expenses of a funeral, and I was almost despairing; my wife however, urged me to pray with her to the Infant Jesus of Prague. The next day the child was out of danger. This gave me new confidence and my wife and I began a novena to the Holy Infant. In a few days we had received a quantity of provisions, which a charitable woman had ordered for us at a store; in the afternoon of the same day another benevolent woman sent us enough food for a month. All this is the more remarkable as we had never asked any person for assistance. But the Divine Infant had more favors in store for us. Before the end of the novena, my wife obtained employment again with kind-hearted people, and throughout the winter we have never wanted for anything, while I have had better food than ever before in my life. It is remarkable, also that we received nearly all our help from Protestants. My health is considerably improved this spring, and I am able to do a little gardening in a small plot of land which a generous neighbor has given us for this purpose. I hope to be quite well in a short time, if the present improvement continues. I feel quite certain the God sent us these numerous afflictions for our own good and the greater honor of the Infant Jesus."

# 13 Conclusion

Christian reader, may these numerous instances of the divine love of the generous bounty of the Infant Jesus produce in your heart a profound and childlike spirit of devotion to His holy infancy. In business troubles, in domestic trials, in sickness of body or soul, hasten to the Infant Jesus of Prague, make Him your confidant, pray to Him with all the fervor of your heart, and above all place full reliance in His almighty power. Nothing pleases the Little King better than to shower favors on those who apply to Him, not only with piety and fervor, but also with the greatest confidence that He will grant their request. If we expect to be heard, we must pray, not only with the devotion of a saint, but also with the simplicity of a child.

Strive also to make the Infant Jesus and His miraculous statue known to those about you, so that everyone may feel for Him a real and lively devotion. He is anxious and very willing to help; but He wants us to apply to Him before He will grant relief.

Sweet and merciful Infant Jesus! Could we but relate all the wonders of Thy power and goodness! Bless at least these few pages, written for Thy greater honor and glory. May they assist in making Thee better known and instilling the devotion to Thy miraculous statue in the hearts of all men! "Peaceful King, employ Thy graces and Thy charms to gain the love of men, and through the sweetness of Thy divine infancy, establish throughout the world Thy happy and blissful reign."

# Prayers.

## Daily Prayers to the Infant Jesus
(to be recited during a novena)

O Almighty God, in the form of a little child! Make me, prostrate at the feet of Thy miraculous image, worthy to meditate on Thy greatness and power, Thy goodness and mercy, and Thy majesty as God and man.

O Divine Infant! With the most profound reverence I contemplate Thy divine *countenance,* shedding its gentle and forgiving light like the sun on good and bad. Deign, ye friendly eyes of my Jesus, to cast one look of grace upon me, and to give my eyes sincere tears of repentance, that on judgment day, they need not fear Thy looks of righteous anger.

O sweetest Jesus! Filled with admiration I praise Thy holy *lip*, filled with heavenly wisdom and uttering words of grace for the remission of sins. Lest, however, Thy divine lips might one day be forced to pronounce the sentence of condemnation on me on account of my own words, I beseech Thee, O Lord, place a seal upon my lips, so that they may never be opened to utter an uncharitable opinion or a sinful word; may I ever preserve Thy truth and Thy love in my heart and upon my tongue.

O merciful Infant! With pious fervor I kiss Thy most holy *hands*, which Thou extendest to hold the entire world in Thy loving embrace. I venerate Thy almighty hand, ruling and governing the universe, and I implore Thee to direct all our works to Thy own honor, and to let Thy right hand be ever extended in blessing over Thy worshippers who confidently pray to Thee.

All hail, ye blessed *feet* of my Redeemer, that have brought peace to the world! What innumerable painful steps you did make during thirty-three years, wearying and bruising yourselves for love of me! I thank Thee a thousand times, O Infant Jesus and I beg of Thee always to direct my feet on the straight road to Thyself, who art the way, the truth and the life.

O most loving *heart* of my Jesus! I greet Thee as many thousand times as Thou didst beat for my salvation. I offer up to my heavenly Father all the flames of divine love burning within Thee. Alas, how ashamed must I not feel at the coldness of my own heart, which only with great difficulty and on rare occasions can excite in itself a proper ardor in return for Thy bountiful love! Take away, O Lord, this cold heart of mine and give me one like Thine own, that I may in future love Thee with a love as warm and glowing as Thine own.

O my most amiable Jesus! Who becamest an *infant* for my sake, endow me, I pray Thee, with the innocence, the humility, and the simplicity of those young souls whom Thou didst call with the words: "Suffer little children to come unto Me, for theirs is the kingdom of heaven."

The beauty of Thy countenance, the sweet expression of Thy eyes, Thy smiling lips, Thy love-inflamed heart, O most beautiful Infant Jesus, excite in me the firm confidence that my hopes will not be disappointed, but that my prayers will find a gracious hearing with Thee, who with the Father and the Holy Ghost livest and reignest One God, world without end. Amen.

# Litany of the Miraculous Infant of Prague

(for private devotion)

Lord, have mercy.
Christ, have mercy.
Lord, have mercy.
Christ, hear us.
*Christ Graciously hear us.*
God the Father of Heaven, Have mercy on us.
God, the Son, Redeemer of the world, Have mercy on us.
God the Holy Ghost, Have mercy on us.
O miraculous Infant Jesus, Have mercy on us.
Infant Jesus, true God and Lord, Have mercy on us.
Infant Jesus, Whose omnipotence is manifested in a wonderful manner, Have mercy on us.
Infant Jesus, Whose wisdom searches our hearts and minds, Have mercy on us.
Infant Jesus, Whose goodness continually inclines to aid us, Have mercy on us.
Infant Jesus, Whose providence leads us to our last end and destiny, Have mercy on us.
Infant Jesus, Whose truth enlightens the darkness of our hearts, Have mercy on us.
Infant Jesus, Whose generosity enriches our poverty, Have mercy on us.
Infant Jesus, Whose friendship consoles the afflicted, Have mercy on us.
Infant Jesus, Whose mercy forgives our sins, Have mercy on us.
Infant Jesus, Whose strength invigorates us, Have mercy on us.
Infant Jesus, Whose power turns away all evils, Have mercy on us.
Infant Jesus, Whose justice deters us from sin, Have mercy

## Devotion to the Miraculous Infant Jesus of Prague

on us.
Infant Jesus, Whose power conquers Hell, Have mercy on us.
Infant Jesus, Whose lovely countenance attracts our hearts, Have mercy on us.
Infant Jesus, Whose greatness holds the universe in its hand, Have mercy on us.
Infant Jesus, Whose miraculous hand raised in benediction fills us with all blessings, Have mercy on us.
Infant Jesus, Whose glory fills the whole world,
Be merciful, Spare us O Jesus.
Be merciful, Graciously hear us, O Jesus.
From all evil, Deliver us, O Jesus.
From all sin, Deliver us, O Jesus.
From all distrust of Thy infinite goodness, Deliver us, O Jesus.
From all doubts in Thy power of miracles, Deliver us, O Jesus.
From all lukewarmness in Thy veneration, Deliver us, O Jesus.
From all trials and misfortunes, Deliver us, O Jesus.
Through the mysteries of Thy holy Childhood, Deliver us, O Jesus.
Through the intercession of Mary, Thy Virgin Mother and St. Joseph Thy foster father, We beseech Thee, hear us.
That Thou wouldst pardon us, We beseech Thee, hear us.
That Thou wouldst bring us to true repentance, We beseech Thee, hear us.
That Thou wouldst preserve and increase in us love and devotion to Thy sacred Infancy, We beseech Thee, hear us.
That Thou wouldst never withdraw Thy miraculous hand from us, We beseech Thee, hear us.
That Thou wouldst keep us mindful of Thy numberless benefits, We beseech Thee, hear us.
That Thou wouldst inflame us more and more with love for Thy Sacred Heart, We beseech Thee, hear us.
That Thou wouldst graciously hear all who call upon Thee

with confidence, We beseech Thee, hear us.
That Thou wouldst preserve our country in peace,
We beseech Thee, hear us.
That Thou wouldst free us from all impending evils,
We beseech Thee, hear us.
That Thou wouldst give eternal life to all who act
generously toward Thee, We beseech Thee, hear us.
That Thou wouldst pronounce a merciful sentence on us
at the judgement, We beseech Thee, hear us.
That Thou wouldst in Thy miraculous Image remain our
consoling refuge, We beseech Thee, hear us.
Jesus, Son of God and of Mary, We beseech Thee, hear us.
Lamb of God, Who takest away the sins of the world,
Spare us, O Jesus.
Lamb of God, Who takest away the sins of the world,
Graciously hear us, O Jesus.
Lamb of God Who takest away the sins of the world,
Have mercy on us.

V. Infant Jesus, hear us.
R. Infant Jesus, graciously hear us.

## OUR FATHER

Our Father, Who art in Heaven, hallowed be Thy Name. Thy Kingdom come. Thy Will be done, on earth, as it is in Heaven. Give us this day our daily bread and forgive us our trespasses as we forgive those who trespass against us; and lead us not into temptation, but deliver us from evil. Amen.

Let us pray.

O Miraculous Infant Jesus, prostrate before Thy sacred Image, we beseech Thee to cast a merciful look on our troubled hearts. Let Thy tender Heart, so inclined to pity, be softened at our prayers, and grant us that grace for which we ardently implore Thee. Take from us all affliction and despair, all trials and misfortunes with which we are laden. For Thy sacred Infancy's sake hear our prayers and send us consolation and aid, that we may praise Thee, with the Father and the Holy Ghost, forever and ever. Amen.

## Prayers for a Novena to the Infant Jesus

1. Eternal Father, I offer to Thy honor and glory, for my eternal salvation and for the salvation of the whole world, the mystery of the birth of our Divine Saviour.

Glory be to the Father, and to the Son and to the Holy Spirit, as it was in the beginning, is now and ever shall be, world without end, Amen.

2. Eternal Father, I offer to Thy honor and glory, and for my eternal salvation, the sufferings of the most holy Virgin and of St. Joseph, in that long and weary journey from Nazareth to Bethlehem. I offer Thee the sorrows of their hearts when they found no place wherein to shelter themselves when the Saviour of the world was born.

Glory be to the Father, and to the Son and to the Holy Spirit, as it was in the beginning, is now and ever shall be, world without end, Amen.

3. Eternal Father, I offer to Thy honor and glory, and for my eternal salvation, the sufferings of Jesus in the stable where He was born, the cold He suffered, the swaddling clothes which bound him, the tears He shed and His tender infant cries.

Glory be to the Father, and to the Son and to the Holy Spirit, as it was in the beginning, is now and ever shall be, world without end, Amen.

4. Eternal Father, I offer to Thy honor and glory, and for my eternal salvation, the pain which the Holy Child Jesus felt in His tender Body when He submitted to circumcision. I offer Thee that Precious Blood which then for the first time, He shed for the salvation of the whole human race.

Glory be to the Father, and to the Son and to the Holy Spirit, as it was in the beginning, is now and ever shall be, world without end, Amen.

5. Eternal Father, I offer to Thy honor and glory, and for my eternal salvation, the humility, mortification, patience, charity, all the virtues of the child Jesus; and I thank Thee, I love Thee, and I bless Thee without end for the ineffable mystery of the Incarnation of the Divine Word.

Glory be to the Father, and to the Son and to the Holy Spirit, as it was in the beginning, is now and ever shall be, world without end, Amen.

V. The Word was made Flesh,
R. And dwelt among us.

*Let us pray,*

O God, whose only-begotten Son was made manifest in the substance of our flesh; grant, we beseech Thee, that through Him, whom we acknowledge to be like unto ourselves, our souls may be inwardly renewed.
Who liveth and reigneth with Thee for ever and ever. Amen.

*An indulgence of one year to all who, on any of the nine days preceding the twenty-fifth of each month, shall recite the above prayers.—Pope Pius IX., Sept. 23, 1846*

# PRAYERS TO BE RECITED BY A SICK PERSON

O merciful Infant Jesus, I know of Thy miraculous deeds to the sick. How many diseases Thou didst cure during Thy blessed life on earth, and how many worshippers of Thy miraculous image ascribe to Thee their recovery and deliverance from most painful and hopeless maladies! I know, indeed, that a sinner like me has merited his suffering and has no right to ask for favors. But, in view of the innumerable graces, and miraculous cures granted even to the greatest sinners through the veneration of Thy holy infancy, particularly in the miraculous statue of Prague or in representations of it, I exclaim with the greatest assurance: O most loving, most pitiful Infant Jesus, Thou canst cure me if Thou wilt! Do not hesitate, O Heavenly Physician, if it be Thy will that I recover again from this present illness; extend Thy most holy hands and by Thy divine power take away all pain and infirmity, so that my recovery may be due not to natural remedies, but to Thee alone. If, however, Thou in Thy inscrutable wisdom hast determined otherwise, then at least restore my soul to perfect health, fill me with heavenly consolation and blessing, that I may be like to Thee, O Jesus, in my suffering, and may on my sick-bed glorify Thy providence, until Thou, by the death of the body, bestowest on me eternal life. Amen.

## PRAYER FOR A HAPPY DEATH

O precious Infant Jesus! I approach Thee now to ask most devoutly for a happy death. When my last moment draws nigh, then come Thou to me in the holy Viaticum; remain near me, bring Thy Virgin Mother and St. Joseph with Thee. Alleviate my sufferings, banish my fear, let me valiantly overcome all temptations, and give me grace willingly to offer up my life as a satisfaction for my sins, in the expectation of everlasting bliss in heaven. In this way I shall be able to gain the special indulgences for the moment of death, the last graces of holy mother Church. Bless me with Thy own divine hands when the priest or any other charitable Samaritan blesses me!

Thou didst live and suffer 12,045 days on this earth, Thou didst labor 289,080 hours for my salvation, and then Thou didst die poor, abandoned, despised, and scoffed at by the world.

By Thy agony in the garden and on the cross, and by all the blood which Thou didst shed, I beseech Thee, grant that my last hour may be happy. But, on account of my tepidity in doing penance and my indifference in gaining indulgences, I fear I shall have to suffer for a long time in purgatory. There I can do nothing for myself, and I shall be dependent entirely on the mediation of others. The dead are, however, soon forgotten. Therefore, my most loving Jesus, I beg Thee even now, by the innocence of Thy holy infancy, liberate me, when I, abandoned and alone, am suffering the torments of purgatory.

With this intention I offer Thy heavenly Father all Thy bitter suffering, the contumely and scoffing, the contempt and abandonment, the terrible agony, all the merits of Thy saints, and all of the Holy Masses that shall be said to the last day. May Thy most precious blood save me when I am weeping in purgatory; may its bountiful streams extinguish the flames that envelop me.

O dear Mother of God, Lady of Perpetual Help, St. Joseph, St. Barbara, my guardian angel, and all my dear patron saints, pray for me. Amen.

## PRAYER OF THANKSGIVING FOR GRACES RECEIVED FROM THE INFANT JESUS OF PRAGUE

I prostrate myself before Thy holy image, O most gracious Infant Jesus, to offer Thee my most fervent thanks for the blessings Thou hast bestowed on me. I shall incessantly praise Thy ineffable mercy and confess that Thou alone art my God, my helper, and my protector. Henceforth my entire confidence shall be placed in Thee; everywhere will I proclaim aloud Thy mercy and generosity, so that Thy great love and the great deeds which Thou performest through this miraculous image may be acknowledged by all. May devotion to Thy holy infancy extend more and more in the hearts of all Christians, and may all who experience Thy assistance persevere with me in showing unceasing gratitude to Thy most holy infancy to which be praise and glory for all eternity. Amen.

## ACT OF CONSECRATION TO THE HOLY CHILD JESUS

O most sweet Child Jesus, who hath so liberally given Thyself to us, I prostrate myself at Thy feet, and under the protection of Thy Immaculate Mother, the ever-Blessed Virgin, and Thy Foster-Father, St. Joseph, I consecrate to Thee my heart, my soul, and my whole being; and I resolve henceforth to love and serve Thee without reserve. Deign,

O Divine Child, to make me feel the Almighty power hidden under Thy littleness and Humility. May Thy spirit of Poverty, of Divine Purity, of Simplicity and of Perfect Obedience descend upon me and upon all who render Thee homage and invoke Thy holy Name. Amen

# Appendix

A Wonderful Incident at Hastings-on-the-Hudson.

A letter received by the publisher from Hastings-on-Hudson, relates the following remarkable incident connected with our present Devotion:

Mrs. H., the mother of the writer, after having been a constant invalid for thirty-five years, finally died in her chair, surrounded by her four children, on July 22nd, 1898. During the last four years of her illness her form had become bent over to such an extent, that it was only by kneeling down that one could see her face, and that when her remains were placed on a bed, the body from the shoulders upward would not touch the pillows. Full of affection and reverence for their venerable mother, her children were much grieved over this deformity of her body. They asked both the priest and the medical doctor if the remains could by any means be straightened. But both answered that there was no natural remedy for it. More saddened, but not disheartened by this answer, one of the daughters, a religious who had always entertained great devotion to the Infant of Prague, took a picture of the Divine Infant and placed it on the head of her beloved mother, saying, whilst the others were pleading with her, "Dear Infant of Prague, You never refused me anything I have asked of You, help us in our petition and I will promote devotion to You." Suddenly the head trembled in her hands and the body became perfectly straightened. The doctor happened to call a few hours later, and when the body was shown to him, he was amazed, and at once asked for the name of the undertaker who had been so skillful as to bring about such wonderful transformation. When informed that no undertaker had touched or seen the remains up to that moment, unable to conceal his surprise, he exclaimed: "This is the most wonderful thing I have ever seen." A photographic picture of the dead body, showing the perfectly straightened form of the old lady, remains in the possession of the grateful witnesses of this wonderful incident.

# PRAYER OF THE REV. P. CYRILLUS A MATRE DEI, THE FIRST AND MOST DEVOTED VENERATOR OF THE MIRACULOUS INFANT JESUS OF PRAGUE

Jesus! Unto Thee I flee,
Through Thy Mother praying Thee
In my need to succor me.
Truly, I believe of Thee
God Thou art with strength to shield me
Full of trust I hope of Thee
Thou Thy grace wilt give to me;
All my heart I give to Thee,
Therefore, of my sins repent me;
From them breaking, I beseech Thee,
Jesus! From their bonds to free me.
Firm my purpose is to mend me,
Never more will I grieve Thee.
Wholly unto Thee I give me,
Patiently to suffer for Thee,
Thee to serve eternally.
And my neighbor, like to me
I will love, for love of Thee,
Little Jesus, I beseech Thee,
In my need to succor me,
That one day I may enjoy Thee,
Save with Joseph, and with Mary,
And angels all, eternally. Amen

Printed in Great Britain
by Amazon